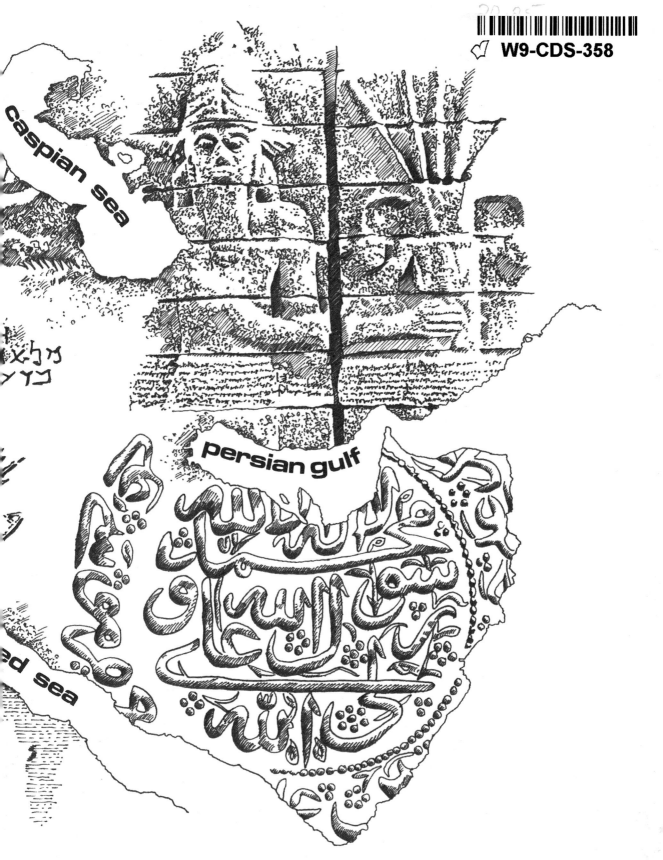

caspian sea

persian gulf

ed sea

Signs,
Letters,
Words

W. John Hackwell

Signs, Letters, Words

Archaeology Discovers Writing

Charles Scribner's Sons • New York

Charles Scribner's Sons Books for Young Readers
Macmillan Publishing Company
866 Third Avenue, New York, NY 10022
Collier Macmillan Canada, Inc.

Printed in the United States of America

First Edition   10 9 8 7 6 5 4 3 2 1

Library of Congress Cataloging-in-Publication Data
Hackwell, W. John   Signs, letters, words.
    Includes index.
    Summary: A history of writing as put together from archaeological evidence.
    1. Writing—History—Juvenile literature.
2. Archaeology—Juvenile literature.
[1. Writing—History.   2. Archaeology]   I. Title.
Z40.H33 1987   652'.1   86-26237
ISBN 0-684-18807-4

Contents

1 · *Before Writing*

At first glance writing seems simple, especially since most of us mastered basic sentences at a very early age. We have long forgotten the attention we had to pay to the order of the letters or the left-to-right orientation of words, let alone the sound-matching and sound-blending that seemed to coincide so naturally with the development of writing skills. Looking back, it seems to us that we moved with incredible speed from the cries of infancy to the complex process of writing good sentences.

In fact, writing is extremely complex. It not only involves a series of deliberate actions by which the writer moves a pen or pencil across a suitable surface. The marks that are left on that surface must be understood by others who have learned the rules of structure and orderliness associated with them. Such marks are called conventional signs.

Conventional signs are clearly recognizable by all users of

1

writing systems such as the English alphabet. Alphabetic writing is the most widespread system of writing today, although in the Orient non-alphabetical systems, such as Chinese and Japanese, are still in use. Oriental writing is based on signs that represent entire words or syllables, and while its origins can be traced to the ancient Near East, such word-syllable systems were in use before the invention of the alphabet.

During this century dedicated archaeologists, historians, and paleographers (students of ancient writing) have pieced together some of the important steps in the five-thousand-year history of writing.

In our society, literacy is taken for granted, but the ancient world was at first without writing. In such a setting we must begin our story of writing.

We can assume that ancient humans initially satisfied their desire to communicate through speech, gesture, and visible symbols. Speech was the means by which humans entered into an intellectual relationship with their environment. For the ancients, a word or a concept was a means of ordering events and ideas, as well as a bridge for communication.

Speech was also a way of gaining mastery and influence. In the ancient Near East a word was widely regarded not as just a bearer of meaningful content, but often as a power in casting spells or curses or in bestowing blessings believed to influence even the natural world. A curse, in the form of a baleful word, could penetrate a person and bring destruction by spreading outward from within. A blessing was thought to bring fertility in man, livestock, and lands.

Speech has major limitations, however, and preliterate people would have found it difficult to think in abstract propositions or to conserve and classify ideas. They probably longed for a way to communicate more adequately. We may assume that this desire eventually led to the development of writing.

Before writing, the accumulated knowledge of human experience mainly involved memorizing names, territorial contracts, clan histories, extensive genealogies, and important tribal myths. Thus the knowledge transmitted was limited by the memories of individuals and was subject to immediate loss due to the brevity and fragility of human life.

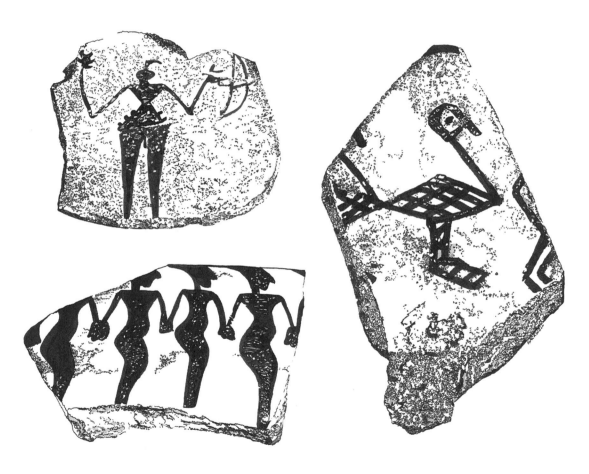

Painted pottery preceded writing. This broken painted pottery, with strong black designs—an archer, dancers, and a decorated bird—dates to 4000 B.C.

3

The accumulation of knowledge in an ancient group also tended to be localized. Knowledge was based on the limited experience of a tribe or clan within a specific geographical location.

Interchange between geographically isolated clans in the preliterate world occurred when such clans were forced to go beyond their well-defined territorial boundaries in times of famine or war. In this way they would eventually return to their homeland with knowledge gained during the journey.

Gesture is a means of visible communication closely associated with speech. In preliterate times many gestures had their origins in family bonds of kinship. The laying on of hands, raising hands in the air, putting a hand on another person's thigh—all had a highly symbolic meaning related to blessing.

Eating and drinking were also visible symbols in the preliterate world. Meals were often formal acts of private or public fellowship. Families and clans believed that they received a share in divine power through the common meal. Peace treaties and covenants were sealed with a meal, and table fellowship meant granting forgiveness, protection, and peace.

In the ancient world pictures were the forerunners of writing. Preliterate paintings are artistic representations that visually suggest ideas or depict events, but they are not writing. They communicate visually, but they are self-contained compositions rather than a system of conventional symbols.

Long before writing, stones were used as another form of visual communication. While the precise archaeological context of these stones is rarely known, their importance to the preliterate world cannot be overlooked. Wandering nomads often built an altar or pillar of stones to commemorate an occasion or a religious practice. Stones were also used to mark the memory of a dead person or to signify a legal relationship between two or more individuals. The most common examples discovered by archaeologists are boundary or treaty stones.

Stones as instruments of cult in some way represented worshipers in a sacred place. A row of stones, for instance, suggests that individuals have a permanent place in the presence of the deity. Such stones have been found with raised hands carved on their surfaces.

Mankind's transition from cave dweller to village settler to city dweller spans thousands of years. The development of writing seems to have been concurrent with the sociological changes that resulted from such transitions.

2 · The Invention of Writing in Mesopotamia

Once the people of Mesopotamia had left their rock shelters to build the first villages (variously dated by archaeologists as between 15,000 and 8000 B.C.), they shaped tiny clay tokens for recording property ownership. This development resulted when nomadic people began to live in crowded village communities, thus abandoning a life of hunting and gathering food to take up the more restricting and organized activities of caring for domestic animals and growing crops. Property ownership and other transactions apparently contributed to the use of tokens in record keeping.

Clay tokens were made in a variety of shapes and sizes, and some archaeologists believe that the different shapes and markings of the tokens enabled them to be used as vouchers or receipts for various goods and perhaps served as title deeds in property transactions.

Tokens were stored and carried in fabric or leather bags, but such organic materials have long since disintegrated. Tokens were also kept inside clay envelopes, and some of these have survived. It is this latter feature that brings us to the invention of writing in Mesopotamia.

In order to know exactly which tokens were encased in a clay envelope the owner marked the exterior of the damp clay with a number of symbols. Once it was realized that the markings on the envelope were virtually duplicating those on the tokens, these latter items went rapidly out of use. It was this practice in particular that later influenced the development of true writing—for writing began on envelope-shaped clay tablets.

The oldest pictographic writing system was used in the first cities that developed in southern Mesopotamia (modern Iraq) between 3500 and 3100 B.C. The symbols consisted of abstract and picturelike signs cut into tiny pillow-shaped clay tablets and linked together in linear fashion. Remarkably, archaeologists have discovered that these abstract forms are similar in appearance not only to pictures and designs to be found on preliterate pottery, but also to many of the clay tokens.

Clay tokens were shaped like discs, cones, cylinders, triangles, and rectangles—exactly the signs used in the later pictographic writing. Markings on the tokens themselves, such as a cross or diagonal lines, also appear frequently in the earliest writing systems.

The choice of clay as the writing material and the presence of a variety of abstract signs once used on tokens, seems to confirm that the development of pictographic writing in Mesopotamia was influenced directly by these tiny clay tokens.

From Pictographs to Wedge-shaped Writing

The earliest known writing system began near the Tigris and Euphrates rivers in southern Mesopotamia. The Sumerians, in-

This is an illustration of a decorated ceramic cup discovered in the Necropolis at Susa (3200 B.C.). Note the three comblike motifs and the center triangle enclosing the triple cross. Such artistic forms resemble aspects of the cuneiform script.

ventors of the wheel and the arch, lived in the southern part of this region.

The invention of writing coincided with the development of the cities of Sumer. Dense city populations required more intricate social organizations than those of the seminomadic cave dwellers. Urban dwellers built defensive walls for increased security and monumental buildings, such as temples and palaces. The production of food through irrigation also demanded a high degree of cooperation and interdependence—to say nothing of the need for effective economic record keeping.

Since life in Mesopotamia centered around the temples, such economic record keeping was probably the function of the priests. Indeed, some archaeologists have suggested that the invention of writing was the result of a demand for more efficient recording than the clay tokens offered. Perhaps it was the priests who invented the idea.

German archaeologists working in the Sumerian city of Uruk (modern Warka) found the earliest evidence of writing. These excavations recovered convex clay tablets inscribed with linear picturelike signs. The signs on these Uruk tablets represent persons or objects and sometimes the name of the person or object.

A drawing of a clay tablet (early third millennium B.C.) from the city of Uruk in Mesopotamia illustrates the earliest stages of pictographic writing.

9

Such signs that represent words are called logograms. Eventually, however, the Sumerians began to associate a sign with a syllable, thus permitting words of more than one syllable to be written with a series of signs. In addition to this development, some signs, called determinatives, were used as indicators to aid in the interpretation of other signs.

With this word-syllable-determinative system the Sumerians were able to write their language with greater ease and accuracy than if they had written with logograms alone, even though their system required almost two thousand independent signs. Obviously such a system could be learned and used only by a limited number of specially skilled people.

The Sumerians were interested in the exploration of units of time, for life revolved around their seasonal and annual festivals. To faciiitate this they devised a numerical system of reckoning time that was related to the base of sixty. The sixty minutes in an hour is a legacy of that sexigesimal system.

In a very short space of time these Sumerian signs lost their pictorial appearance altogether and became more abstract and linear.

The majority of early tablets discovered in Mesopotamia were written in the Sumerian language. This script is illustrated on this inscribed stone, which was written for the Sumerian ruler Ur-Nanshe. Discovered at Tello in Iraq, the stone dates to 2500 B.C.

This illustration of an early Sumerian stone tablet (from Lagash, about 2500 B.C.) records a land sale in an early style of cuneiform. Each portion of the transaction is marked off by a little box. Such divisions, made by the ancient scribe, are of great help to the decipherer.

Signs eventually came to represent sounds rather than objects. Once this occurs their appearance can be streamlined without losing readability, so long as all users of the system know what is happening.

Now that signs represented sounds rather than objects, the scribes could write at high speed. They also invented a writing instrument from a sharpened reed, and it is this latter development that gave its name to Mesopotamian wedge-shaped writing: cuneiform (literally meaning "reed-form").

Eventually the scribes pressed the signs on the damp clay tablets in a uniform direction, a habit that made the use of the reed stylus easier. Many complex signs were eliminated as more sharp-edged versions were much easier and quicker to execute.

Cuneiform eventually became exceptionally precise, even though scripts reflect the scribe's individual style and personality. Scripts on some tablets have been quite skillfully executed while others appear rather clumsy, as if rushed. When stone monuments, precious metals, or objects were inscribed, the script was more formal than on the everyday tablets and often reflected long outmoded signs.

Writing was employed for a variety of purposes in ancient Mesopotamia. Thousands of tablets have been recovered that deal with routine matters such as buying and selling, fishing and hunting. Many objects such as bowls, statues, and the stone pillars or slabs known as stelae bear inscriptions that dedicate the object to religious or political use.

This is a bronze goblet inscribed with the name Lilul, King of Akkad. The chief interest of this goblet is the inscription in very early cuneiform.

This is an illustration of an Old Assyrian tablet still enclosed in the clay envelope in which it was to have been sent. On the envelope are the impressions made by rolling three cylinder seals. There is a cuneiform inscription between the seal impressions.

The Sumerians even invented the letter in the envelope. Archaeologists have discovered ancient archives that contain hundreds of clay tablets enclosed within clay envelopes that either duplicate or summarize the encased text.

Ownership seals were often pressed onto the envelope when the clay was damp to indicate the originator of the text or simply to witness to its veracity. Jar lids, boxes, and doors were often sealed with clay and then impressed with a cylinder seal.

In ancient Mesopotamia two devices evolved to facilitate the transfer of goods and services. One was writing, and the second was cylinder sealing. Seals were used to ensure the veracity of a shipment of goods. This is an illustration of a cylinder seal impression from Mesopotamia.

The Diffusion of Cuneiform

The trend toward a standard cuneiform text resulted from the dominance of Sumerian centers like Ur, Kish, and Nippur and the diffusion of that culture's influence.

Cuneiform spread west into Egypt and east into the region of modern Iran where a script known as proto-Elamite evolved and continued on a separate line of development. Cuneiform has also been found to the north in Syria at Mari on the Euphrates and at Ebla, farther to the west. The Ebla script is identical to the cuneiform of the Sumerians at Kish, and yet the people of Ebla were transcribing their own Semitic language.

After 2000 B.C. war, politics, and commerce further contributed to the spread of the cuneiform script over an ever wider geographical area. By this time distinctive scripts had developed

This illustration of a silver Paleo-Elamite vase from Marudasht, near Persepolis, has a band of script at the level of the head. These are the hieroglyphic characters of the early Elamites (third millennium B.C.).

in Mesopotamia, in Babylonia in the south and Assyria in the north—two areas where major archives have been recovered.

Between 1550 and 1200 B.C. Akkadian and other local languages were written in the wedge-shaped cuneiform script at the Hittite, Assyrian, Elamite, and Egyptian courts. Extensive archives have been excavated at Ugarit on the Mediterranean coast of Syria, Tell el Amarna in Egypt, at various Hittite centers, and recently in north-central Syria.

This inscription, on a statue that was dedicated in the temple of Ishtar at Mari, was inscribed in the Akkadian language. The sign values were written from right to left. The translation reads: "Statue of Ebihil, the steward, dedicated to the virile Ishtar."

16

This tablet (2900 B.C.) bears an Elamite inscription. The script was not borrowed from Sumer but invented at ancient Susa.

This cuneiform system, although radically modified, became an international form of writing and survived the Assyrian, neo-Babylonian, and Persian empires. It was still in use long after the conquests of Alexander the Great and didn't go out of fashion until the first century A.D.

It wasn't until the eighteenth century that the western world became interested in discovering the original intent and meaning of the various cuneiform scripts. An inscription on the tomb of Darius the First (in modern Iran) written in Elamite, Old Persian, and Babylonian, provided the key to its decipherment. In 1885 archaeologist Henry Rawlinson, with the help of others, used his working knowledge of modern Persian to obtain an understanding of cuneiform.

This is an illustration of a marble statue of Alexander the Great, who founded an empire that shared the cultural heritage of the Greeks. The use of a common language helped erase old hatreds and national rivalries.

18

Since the pioneering days of Henry Rawlinson, literally thousands of cuneiform tablets, as well as cylinder seals and monumental texts, have been translated into English. While the vast majority are only repetitive economic records, even they have helped archaeologists identify an ancient trade route or hitherto unknown village. Other texts have brought us face to face with ancient kings such as Darius the Great, Artaxerxes, Assurbanipal, or Nebuchadnezzar. Still others describe complex and sensitive law codes.

Of equal importance, however, the cuneiform tablets reveal that the ancients of Mesopotamia were challenged by the deepest concerns of humanity, such as the origin of life and the problems associated with pain and suffering.

While it may not be true to say that history began at Sumer, archaeology has shown that as the inventors of writing the Sumerians have given to humanity perhaps the greatest intellectual gift of all time.

3 · Writing in Ancient Egypt

The ancient inhabitants along the Nile had produced many abstract designs prior to the invention of writing. These artistic signs were painted on pottery and provided later scribes with a major source for writing.

Writing actually commenced in Egypt about 3100 B.C., during the same period that it appeared in Mesopotamia. Since its grammatical principles were almost identical to those of cuneiform, many have assumed that the Egyptians borrowed the system from their faraway neighbors in Sumer.

While this question will always remain controversial, archaeology has shown that Egypt and Mesopotamia did enjoy extensive economic contact, which coincided with the appearance of writing. Certainly the Egyptians borrowed the concept of cylinder sealing from Sumer, but one cannot escape the fact that unlike Mesopotamia ancient Egyptian writing reflects the cultural context of a single isolated race.

The earliest style of ancient Egyptian writing is called hieroglyphics, from the Greek term meaning "sacred inscriptions." The Egyptians, like other ancient literate societies, associated writing with the divine.

Hieroglyphic symbols are unmistakably pictorial. Some signs are ideograms representing an object, an action, or an idea. A bird sign, for instance, could represent the bird itself or simply ideas of "flight" or "speed." Such signs could also represent the

The creative inhabitants along the Nile valley had produced a number of signs in the preliterate period that were artistic representations on painted pottery, as this illustration of a pre-Dynastic jar reveals. Thus, older artistic forms provided a major source for the hieroglyphic signs.

21

sounds of one or more consonants. When used in this way they are called phonograms. Still other pictorial signs stood for words that had no physical object to represent them.

Hieroglyphics therefore could have been rather confusing since a single sign not only could be read in several different ways but also could have diverse meanings. Like the Mesopotamians before them, the ancient Egyptians solved this problem by utilizing a class of identifier signs or ideograms to specify the exact intention of the word. For example, a drawing of a man followed by five vertical strokes clearly suggests that "five men" is intended.

The early Egyptian writing system was made cumbersome by the royal scribes, who, rather than adapt, clung to many burdensome conventions. They permitted the script to be written either to the left or the right, for instance, or up or down—often on the same inscription.

Egyptian scribes were, however, innovative in their choice of writing materials, and the forms of their signs were no doubt influenced by such choices. While the Sumerians wrote on soft clay by pressing a sharpened reed or stick into its surface—thereby limiting their script to wedges and lines—the Egyptians wrote with a brush and ink on papyrus sheets made from a water reed that grew in the Nile valley, thus affording great flexibility in style. With such writing instruments at their disposal, scribes were not content to simply outline a bird. They would often draw that sign with intricate detail including feathers, eyes, and beak. In this way hieroglyphs can be said to be an amalgamation of writing and graphics.

While the Sumerians and Egyptians both used cylinder seals and often carved their writing systems on stone, the Egyptians added to this a range of inscribed scarabs made of semiprecious gems.

In 1822 the French linguist Jean François Champollion dramatically established that the perched birds, staring faces, and coiled snakes on the stones of Egypt could form words unrelated to their images. This illustration, based on an inscription from Karnak, includes the royal name of Sesostris I in the rounded frame, or cartouche.

This drawing of a red granite statue of a seated scribe, found in Giza, Egypt, dates to the Old Kingdom (2400 B.C.) and gives an indication of the vital and favored position these persons held in Egyptian social life.

Eventually the Egyptians added a cursive form of hieroglyphs, and by 1778 B.C. its use was well established. When the Greeks conquered Egypt more than a thousand years later, they referred to this script as *hieratic,* meaning "priestly." They thought that it was some form of religious text when in fact decipherment of hieratic confirmed that it was often used for secular texts such as business documents, poems, and short stories.

In the seventh century B.C. a third, and even less pictorial, script appeared. The Greeks called this *demotic*, meaning "popular," since it served a more everyday purpose than either hieroglyphs or hieratic. Demotic looks almost like a scrawl compared to the earlier forms. Actually it is a cursive grouping of two or more originally separate symbols.

Even though the old hieroglyphic system suffered from restricted usage, it continued to be employed until A.D. 400 when, together with hieratic, it was eclipsed by the demotic form. All three, however, declined with the universal acceptance of the Greek language, which was adopted by the Egyptian people in the second century B.C.

To achieve this transition the Egyptians combined twenty-five letters from the Greek with seven signs from the demotic to establish the Coptic alphabet, a script still used today by the Coptic church in Egypt. Prior to this the ancient Egyptians had not

The Egyptians wrote on papyrus made from the pith of plants native to the Nile valley. They used ink and a reed brush to draw their hieroglyphic signs. This illustration depicts the Chester Beatty papyrus, found at Thebes written in the hieratic script.

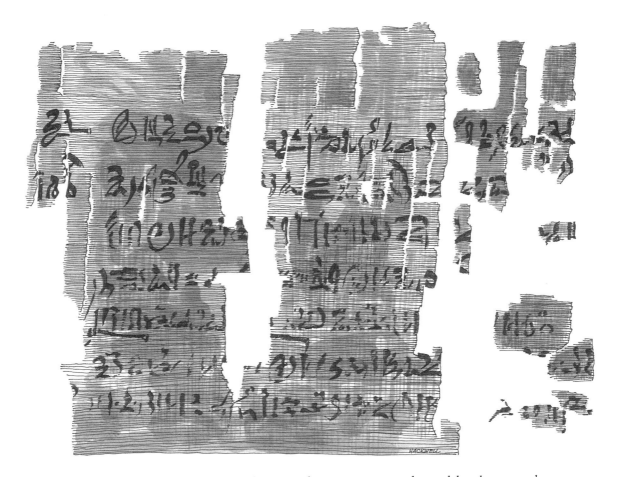

The selection of writing materials in a culture was in part dictated by the natural environment that influenced the availability of materials. When the Chester Beatty papyrus was unrolled it was discovered to be a mythological narrative from the twentieth Egyptian dynasty at Thebes. This illustration shows the fragmented nature of a portion of that papyrus.

constructed an alphabetic system, although they did use a type of alphabet when listing the names of foreign nobles they had captured. This consisted of twenty-seven hieroglyphic signs that, in addition to their normal usage, could be read as individual consonants.

Throughout their long history the Egyptians seemed to resist, or at least to ignore, progress across their borders. They must have known of a revolutionary development taking place in Syria-Palestine where a far less complex alphabetic system of writing was in use. Perhaps the adoption of such a system would have symbolized for the Egyptians a drastic loss of national pride or identity.

By the fifth century A.D., the Egyptian scripts were all but buried and forgotten, although the incredible visual appeal of the scripts continued to fascinate and challenge western explorers and travelers. Speculation about the meaning and intent of hieroglyphs reached its peak in medieval Europe, but it was not until 1799 that the discovery of the Rosetta Stone by members of Napoleon's expeditionary forces to Egypt provided a reliable key to understanding these ancient texts.

The Rosetta Stone is inscribed in three different languages — Greek, hieratic, and hieroglyphs—and several scholars attempted to decipher the text, but it wasn't until 1822 that a brilliant

This is an illustration of papyrus showing the demotic script. It is a part of a contract from 270 B.C.

27

The word Coptic *is directly related to the word* Egypt. *This illustration of a Coptic ostracon (a fragment of pottery or limestone bearing an inscription) is a fine example of that script.*

young Frenchman named Jean François Champollion finally mastered the script.

Since this important beginning, many British, European, and American archaeological teams have uncovered thousands of hieroglyphic inscriptions from one end of Egypt to the other. Today ancient Egyptian history is probably the best known and documented of all, and this magnificent writing system continues to fascinate and influence people all over the world.

4 · Writing in Syria-Palestine

Syria-Palestine was strategically located on the important trade routes that linked the two great civilizations of Egypt and Mesopotamia. Rather than journey directly to Egypt across the vast Arabian desert, the merchants of Sumer went north along the Euphrates River valley, then down the coastal region of what is now Lebanon, Syria, Jordan, and Israel, and then crossed the Sinai peninsula into Egypt.

In ancient times the region of Syria-Palestine was occupied by groups of peoples referred to in the Bible as Canaanites. Living in small fortified urban centers surrounded by fruit trees and crops of cereals and vegetables, they obtained revenue from the foreign commerce along the vital trade routes between Egypt and Mesopotamia.

This was a period of constant change when many dialects were spoken. It was not until 1300 B.C., with the establishment of more central city-states with their public buildings such as palaces, central granaries, and fortifications, that the languages of Phoenician, Hebrew, Ammonite, Moabite, Edomite, and Aramaic can be distinguished.

From the extensive archaeological excavations that have taken place in this region it is clear that the Canaanites not only understood the cuneiform writing system of Mesopotamia and the hieroglyphics of Egypt, they were also familiar with the hieroglyphics of the Hittites to the north, who used their own forms of pictographs as well as the cuneiform of Mesopotamia.

Thanks to their strategic location on the coast, the Canaanites were also familiar with the writing systems of the inhabitants of the Mediterranean islands such as Crete where a linear form of syllable signs was in use as early as 2000 B.C.

The Invention of the Alphabet

The invention of alphabetic writing, which limits the number of signs to thirty or fewer, instead of the hundreds of signs in hieroglyphic or cuneiform writing, is one of the greatest revolutions in the development of human civilization. This ingenious innovation came into being in Syria-Palestine during the second millennium B.C. and is Canaan's greatest contribution to human endeavor.

Although it is quite possible that the alphabet was the result of an invention, it was more likely the next logical step in a process of development. It is easy to understand why it came into being with the Canaanites.

The early Canaanite settlements were not subject to the power of an established priesthood whose writing habits were dominated by the tenacity of tradition, such as existed in both Mesopotamia and Egypt. One can imagine that Canaanite merchants and bureaucrats, frustrated with the time-consuming and com-

This illustration of a royal buttress from Carchemish shows Hittite hiero-glyphs between King Araras (whose head is broken away) and his son Kamanas.

plicated writing systems of their neighbors, may have decided to make improvements in the way to write.

As we have observed, the earliest pictographic writing systems used logograms, then added ideograms, then developed to a stage where many signs stood for spoken words. This latter advance is called phonetization. Once signs represent sounds, there is no need for them to depict physical objects. Thus we found that the Sumerian writing system became abstract and linear.

Archaeologists and experts in ancient Semitic languages expected to find evidence that the users of cuneiform took the next logical step—that of using signs to represent clusters of sounds, called syllables. But such is not the case. The Canaanites appear to have bypassed that concept when they invented the alphabet, for they recognized that speech consisted of basic sounds that could be represented with a very few signs.

The Semitic Alphabet

One of the distinguishing features of Semitic languages is that most words have a common root based on three consonants called a triliteral. These root letters are easily made into nouns or verbs by simply attaching consonants at the beginning or end. This system was so versatile and recognizable that the Canaanite scripts were written with consonants only.

Primitive forms of the Canaanite alphabetic script were discovered almost a century ago by the famous Egyptologist Sir William Flinders Petrie who found them near the Egyptian turquoise mines at Serabit el-Khadem in southern Sinai. The small number of texts and their brevity prevented a thorough decipherment of all the signs. Some archaeologists believe, however, that these inscriptions were written by workers from

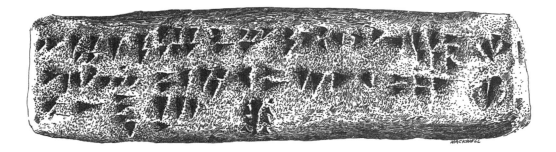

This is a drawing of the Ugarit "ABC" tablet found at Ras Shamra, Syria. It shows the simplest combinations of wedges that the scribes of Ugarit used to form their alphabet. Like the Mesopotamian cuneiform, these signs are written from left to right. They are listed in alphabetical order, the same order that we find in use in Hebrew today and that underlies the order of the letters of our modern English alphabet (1500 B.C.).

Canaan engaged in their trade on behalf of the Egyptians and that they are the earliest forms of the Semitic alphabet so far discovered.

The French archaeological expedition to Ras Shamra in Syria in 1929 uncovered a rich archive of cuneiform alphabetic tablets. Ras Shamra has since proved to be the ancient city of Ugarit that flourished until its destruction in 1200 B.C. These Ugaritic cuneiform tablets included a treasure of west Semitic mythology containing many parallels to the Bible in language, expressions, and content.

The Canaanites at Ugarit not only adopted the Mesopotamian cuneiform, they reduced the number of wedge combinations to form an alphabet. Indeed on one archaeological expedition a tablet was uncovered that lists these signs in alphabetical order. It is the same order that underlies the modern Hebrew and English alphabets.

In the subsequent excavations at Ras Shamra-Ugarit hundreds of tablets written in hieroglyphs, Hittite, Babylonian, and the

The city of Ugarit was destroyed in approximately 1200 B.C. by the incursions of the sea peoples from the west. This proved to be the eclipse also of the cuneiform alphabet. This illustration from the Temple of Ramses III in Egypt depicts the sea peoples as the Egyptians saw them.

scripts of Cyprus and Crete have been recovered, thus confirming the strategic importance of this Canaanite center.

Isolated examples of the Ugaritic alphabet have also been discovered farther south in Israel at Beth-Shemesh, Taanach, and at Mount Tabor where it was discovered inscribed on a copper knife blade. Such discoveries suggest that this cuneiform alphabet enjoyed a brief usage until approximately 1200 B.C. when invasions of sea peoples from the west and other new ethnic elements caused widespread disruption in the region.

While the order of the letters of the Canaanite alphabet was probably established at its very inception, such conventions as the direction of the writing still varied from one city-state to another since each was exhibiting a certain political and cultural independence.

The Canaanite Linear Alphabet

Between 1200 and 900 B.C. a Canaanite linear alphabet was developed. This alphabet was written in Hebrew, Phoenician, Aramaic, and other scripts. By 1050 B.C. the forms of the letters, their stance, and the direction of the writing had been well established.

This is also the period of the first kings of Israel—Saul, David, and Solomon—whose reigns witnessed successive population displacements, ethnic movements, and the destruction of cities and kingdoms, with the result that very few inscriptions from this period have been discovered.

One recent discovery, however, at Isbet Sartah near Tel Aviv, has produced the earliest Hebrew inscription known. Isbet Sartah was a small Israelite village used as a staging area for the Israelites in their battle against the Philistines who were grouped a few miles away at Apheq (1 Samuel 4). The meaning of this

The proto-Canaanite alphabet gave birth to three national scripts—Phoenician, Hebrew, and Aramaic. This drawing of the Kilamuwa inscription illustrates a mixture of the Phoenician and Aramaic languages. The script is Phoenician. Kilamuwa bar-Haya, king of Yadi-Samal, had the inscription cut during his reign in the small city-state in what is now southern Turkey in the late ninth century B.C.

inscription is the subject of much speculation among archaeologists, since the alphabetical signs appear in no logical sequence at all. What is important, however, is that a linear alphabet was in use in Israel as early as the eleventh century B.C..

In 1923 a French expedition discovered the stone coffin of King Ahiram of Tyre, a contemporary of both David and Solomon. The huge sarcophagus contained a Phoenician inscription around the edge of the lid written in a linear alphabet, thus revealing yet another line of development from the earlier Canaanite.

These two examples are among several from the period that confirm the existence of a stabilized linear script written from left to right in horizontal fashion. By this time Syria-Palestine had shaken off all remnants of earlier pictographic writing systems.

The Diffusion of the Canaanite Alphabet

King Solomon died in 931 B.C., and the subsequent division of his empire witnessed not only the development of an independent Israelite script but a period of widespread literacy, even in geographically isolated centers. The Siloam Tunnel inscription of King Hezekiah, various seal impressions, and many inscribed jar handles found in isolated villages all confirm the literacy of the Judean people at the time.

The most significant archaeological evidence for the development of an independent Hebrew script is not to be found in Israel proper but in one of its vassals east of the Jordan River. Here a commemorative stone inscribed with the deeds of the king of ancient Moab reveals the distinctive features of a script

This potsherd from Israel, with marks or letters scratched on its surface, was possibly scribbled by a child. The existence of writing of this type suggests that the people of Judea were literate, even in geographically isolated settlements.

that would remain in Israel for the next four hundred years.

Because organic writing materials tended to perish, ostraca from ancient Israel are of singular importance. Writing on the surfaces of these pottery or limestone fragments has survived in this region while the more frequently used papyrus scrolls have disappeared.

In ancient Israel the art of writing was preserved as a craft by certain families. Archaeological evidence gives an unchanging picture of the scribe, either standing making brief notes or seated on a stool, bench, or floor, with a scroll or codex on his knees. A scribal school was established during the reigns of David and Solomon to train suitable priests, already at the forefront of temple operations, in the art of writing.

In Israel writing took on an unparalleled theological importance, for here the most sacred act of writing concerned an act of God. The Israelites taught that their moral law was inscribed on stone by the very hand of God. They wrote it on their doorposts and on pieces of parchment. For them the written word was a witness having preeminent authority for later generations.

As we have seen, the Canaanite alphabet gave birth to the Phoenician along the Mediterranean coast and to an early form of Hebrew in the central highlands west of the Jordan. This diffusion also continued eastward as the Canaanite alphabet

These illustrations of two seals offer examples of the skills of the seal makers in Israel. The minuscule letters are engraved on carnelian. Both seals date to the late eighth century B.C.

This relief found by archaeologists at Palmyra in Syria depicts the local Aramaic script—a direct descendant of Canaanite.

branched to the early Arabic scripts of the Yemen, Ethiopia, and Egypt.

With the general disruptions that occurred at the end of the thirteenth century B.C., Aramean tribes from the north occupied Syria just as the Israelites were engaged in lightning strikes against several major Canaanite strongholds. Very soon the kingdom of Assyria began to exert its influence in the region, and it adopted Aramaic as the main language of communication with the conquered peoples. Aramaic eventually became the lan-

By 730 B.C. the Hittites had come under the influence of the Arameans and the Assyrians. Such influence is evident in this bas-relief of the king on an Assyrian-type throne. Moreover, the old hieroglyphic script has been replaced by the Aramean language and the Semite alphabetic script. The scribe is holding an Egyptian writing set (box of instruments).

40

guage of the Assyrian and later Babylonian empires. It is thus a matter of historical circumstance that when the Jews were exiled into Babylon in 605 B.C. they began to speak and write in Aramaic and lost all knowledge of the earlier Hebrew form.

Like the Mesopotamians and Egyptians before them, however, the Jews who later left Babylon and returned to their homeland continued to use the older forms for special titles, such as when they wrote the name of God. The discovery of the Dead Sea Scrolls at Qumran written some five hundred years

Among the several scripts that developed from the Aramaic, the script of an Arab tribe that occupied Trans-Jordan from the fourth century B.C. until the Roman period forms a transition from the Aramaic to the Arabic. This is an illustration of one of the very rare Nabataean inscriptions discovered by archaeologists at Petra in Jordan.

later confirms that a few words of the Old Hebrew script were reserved for such purposes. But the language of the general population, even at the time of Christ, was still Aramaic and not Hebrew.

Meanwhile, the Samaritans, who had separated from Israel at roughly the time of the exile into Babylon, continued to use a form of the earlier Hebrew script.

One of the least known scripts that developed from the Aramaic belonged to the Nabataeans, a powerful Arabic tribe who controlled the vital Trans-Jordan trade routes between Syria and Egypt. Establishing a capital at Petra near the Gulf of Aqaba,

This Kufic inscription on a tombstone found in Egypt is typical of this calligraphic method, which placed words in heavy rows. Muslim artists provided innumerable variations of Kufic until it reached full maturity in the eleventh and twelfth centuries.

they built a heavily fortified city that virtually controlled Trans-Jordan from the fourth century B.C. on in to the Roman period. Modern Arabic is descended from this Nabataen script and not from the Old South Arabic of the Yemen.

One of the earliest and most decorative Arabic scripts is the Kufic, which takes its name from the Mesopotamian city of Kufa. While Kufic inscriptions are to be found on tombstones and other similar monuments, the script was also used to transcribe the Koran until the twelfth century A.D. when it was replaced by the even more decorative Arabic.

Since Islam forbade the depiction of the living form, Islamic scribes enhanced the appearance of their books with creative forms of the fluid Arabic alphabet rather than with figural artistic representations. This is an illustration of an Islamic ceramic tile from the nineteenth century A.D. found at Damascus, Syria.

43

While written and spoken Arabic flourished on every continent that opened to Islam, the Hebrew script of the Bible became increasingly difficult to read since the language itself was no longer spoken. To overcome this problem a group of Jewish scholars known as Masoretes, who lived in Tiberius in A.D. 800, developed a series of indicating vowels to preserve the pronunciation of the Hebrew text.

During the fifth through ninth centuries A.D. the Hebrew language was seldom spoken, and precision in reading became a problem. In 800 A.D. the Masoretes, who were scholars living near Tiberius, developed a system of vowel pointing to preserve proper pronunciation for synagogue services. This illustration of a page from a Hebrew Bible (Antwerp 1566) shows the developed Masoretic text of the Renaissance. The dots and dashes under the script represent the vowel pointing system.

This illustration of an eighteenth-century gold medal struck at Tabriz illustrates an example of the later exceptional calligraphy of Islamic tribes.

One of the most intriguing aspects of the history of writing is that two such unrelated alphabets as modern Hebrew and Arabic originated not from the Old Hebrew or Old Arabic (which had in turn derived from the Canaanite) but from the same Aramaic source.

5 · Writing Systems of the Aegean and Europe

The spread of the Semitic alphabet to Europe began in the islands of the eastern Mediterranean and the Aegean seas. Its acceptance and widespread use was not automatic, however, since many nonalphabetical systems were well established.

The Aegean Scripts

Ancient Crete was a thriving civilization early in the third millennium B.C. In several respects it rivaled Mesopotamia and Egypt in the same period. By 2000 B.C. the Minoans were custodians of their own unique pictographic writing system. Unfortunately for modern scholarship, fewer than two hundred pictographs have been tentatively identified, and the language remains a mystery.

Some rather brief but nonetheless important linear scripts from the same period, inscribed on clay, stone, and metal, have also been recovered on the islands of Melos, Crete, and Thera. While their meaning remains a mystery, the signs probably represent the names of objects or a description of property.

From approximately 1450 B.C. another major writing system referred to as Linear B emerged in the region and was used to transcribe the Mycenaean dialect of Greek. Unlike the earlier pictographic systems, it did not contain logograms or determinatives but was a syllabic system used to write Greek

This is an illustration of the "Phaestos Disk" (1700–1550 B.C.) from Phaestos in Crete, a circular clay plaque 6½" in diameter inscribed with 122 hieroglyphs of an as yet undeciphered text. The characters have been stamped rather than drawn onto clay.

This baked clay tablet, written in Linear B script, was the first one discovered in the excavations at Pylos. It gives the distribution of rowers sent to Pleuron in Aetolia. The vertical strokes at the right of each division represent the numbers of men attending from each group. The strokes are preceded by an ideogram representing a man. This script was used by the Mycenaean Greeks on both the mainland and on the island of Crete before 1000 B.C. More than 3,000 of these inscriptions have been recovered.

phonetically. The Linear B tablets consist mostly of administrative and accounting matters involving various commercial transactions. They do have a decimal numerical system, as revealed by signs placed to the right side of the commodity or measure with which they were associated.

The Classical Greek Alphabet

Archaeological evidence suggests that the Greeks borrowed the alphabet from the Phoenicians sometime between 1200 and 800 B.C.

As we have noted earlier, the disruptions that occurred in Syria-Palestine around 1200 B.C. reduced the Phoenicians to a small strip of territory along the coastline where for the next three hundred years they vigorously pursued maritime interests that naturally brought them into close contact with the Greeks.

When we compare the Phoenician and Greek alphabets, it becomes obvious that the Greeks made full use of the alphabet invented by the Phoenicians. For example, the names of the Greek alphabet letters closely resemble those of the Phoenician. The two Greek letters most familiar today, "alpha" and "beta," are derived directly from the Semitic words "aleph" and "beth" and stand for the first two letters of the Greek alphabet. Indeed, the word "alphabet" is simply a combination of those two letters. Other similarities, such as the shape, order, and numerical value of the letters, provide further evidence to suggest such a borrowing.

But the Greeks did not just borrow the Phoenician alphabet; they reinterpreted and adapted it to suit their own particular cultural context. They made deletions and additions to produce an alphabet that worked best for them. In the Phoenician alphabet every word commenced with a consonant; in fact, every sign was a consonant, and this demonstrates how familiar the Phoenicians were with their system. But the Greeks, receiving the alphabet "second hand" as it were, needed to insert vowels to obtain correct pronunciation. (Once we are familiar with English, we could probably read most words with vowels omitted.)

The Greeks further introduced more streamlined writing materials. The Egyptians had used a brush to write on papyrus—obviously an extremely slow and potentially damaging process.

The Greeks made several additions of their own to the alphabet they had adopted from the Phoenicians. Phi ϕ was the earliest new sign developed— as seen on this illustration of a Greek coin (356 B.C.) depicting Philip III of Macedon riding his horse and carrying a palm branch, emblem of victory.

ΚΗΦΙΣΟΦΩΝΠΑΙΑΝΙΕΥΣ
ΕΓΡΑΜΜΑΤΕΥΕ
ΣΑΜΙΟΙΣΟΣΟΙΜΕΤΑΤΟΔΗΜΟΤΟΑΘΗΝΑΙ
ΑΝΕΓΕΝΟΝΤΟ

This is an Attic decree passed in Athens in 405 B.C., conferring Athenian citizenship on the Samians who remained faithful to Athens. Patron goddesses of Athens and Samos shake hands. This stele exhibits the classical Greek monumental script of the day.

51

The Greeks invented the sharp-tipped pen or nib, thus enabling a Greek scribe to double the output possible when using the brush technique. This capacity was further enhanced when the Greeks later introduced parchment.

By 300 B.C. the classical Greek alphabet had replaced those of the small city-states to become the monumental script of this dynamic empire.

Even though thousands of Etruscan inscriptions have been discovered, the language remains undeciphered. Interestingly, the Etruscan texts run from right to left, which suggests that they borrowed the alphabet very early from Phoenicia. An illustration of a brief Etruscan text appears on the lip of this third-century B.C. clay bowl unearthed in Italy.

The Latin Alphabet

While statements concerning the origin and language of the Etruscans have always been tentative, these people were once in Asia Minor as close neighbors of the Phoenicians before they migrated (around 1200 B.C.) from Lydia to the Italian peninsula. It is possible that they obtained the alphabet directly from the Phoenicians. More likely, however, migrating families learned of it from merchants at the bustling Aegean seaports.

Whatever the case, the Etruscans seem to have adopted the alphabet almost as early as the Greeks.

The Etruscans, who form a critical bridge between the Greek and Roman civilizations, are said to be responsible for the transmission of the alphabet to the Romans, who, in turn, developed it into the Latin alphabet.

It was during the second century A.D. that a script for everyday use evolved in which the letters flowed together—probably the result of more flexible pens, more soluble inks, and smoother writing surfaces that would have permitted far greater speed.

Eventually, a minuscule script developed that was used in combination with capital letters. This tradition remains nearly two thousand years later. We begin sentences and commence proper names with capitals and use minuscule script for the rest of our handwriting.

6 · The Spread of the Alphabet

With the conquests of Imperial Rome came the rise to power and influence of the literate Roman Church bishops. As a result, from the Byzantine period onward there was widespread acceptance of the "holy" Latin script.

Eastern Europe and Asia, on the other hand, witnessed the spread of the Cyrillic alphabet. Though different in form from the Latin, Cyrillic is nonetheless anchored in the Greek. Of the forty-three modern Russian Cyrillic signs, at least half derive directly from ninth and tenth century Greek.

After 1492 traveling merchants introduced the Latin alphabet to the peoples of Africa, the Americas, and many of the South Pacific Islands.

The Influence of the Bible

The merchant ships that visited the New World carried their contingents of Christian missionaries, who were dedicated to the task of taking the Bible to these unknown peoples of the sea. Spurred on by their own recently acquired ability to read the King James English Bible, these missionaries believed that Christ's words in Matthew 24—"This Gospel shall go to all the world"—presented them with a divine mandate to adapt the alphabet to hundreds of foreign languages and to translate portions of the Bible into local dialects.

The Phoenician form of the Semitic alphabets influenced the alphabets of the West, developing into the Greek, Etruscan, Latin, and the European scripts. This sketch of a silver double thalers coin from Germany (Johann Georg II of Saxony A.D. 1663–1661) in the Latin (Roman) form helps to illustrate the progress of diffusion westward.

The expansion of the Catholic Church played a major role in the spread of
the Latin language in Western Europe. This drawing of a carved ivory book
cover from A.D. 1050 illustrates that influence.

One intriguing legacy of this endeavor can be observed when one visits a remote highland village in Papua New Guinea today. There it is possible to meet tribal villagers unable to speak a word of English but who have little difficulty in reading aloud portions of the King James Bible.

Such unprecedented dissemination of the alphabet made little impact in China, however. There the grandeur of the Chinese nonalphabetical writing system was to remain as the written communication of the Chinese people.

Paper and the Printing Press

The Chinese had invented paper early in the second century A.D. and maintained a monopoly on its production until the Moslems obtained knowledge of papermaking in A.D. 751, some three hundred and fifty years before it arrived in Europe.

The Chinese also invented movable type. In 1440 Johannes Guttenberg not only adapted this invention in Europe by making letters out of metal, he converted a cheese press to take his letters and produced the printing press. By 1446 Gutenberg had completed his famous printed Bible.

Before printing was invented, medieval scribes had to copy books and manuscripts by hand, word for word. Long hours of tiresome concentration often produced errors. With the introduction of printing, however, spelling and punctuation conventions became standardized, and fewer errors occurred. (To paleographers such scribal errors are of great importance, since the recurrence of an error in different ancient manuscripts helps them to determine the date and source of a document.)

In 1867 Christopher Sholes invented the typewriter; this also helped standardize conventions and reduce errors. Now we have word processors with computerized memories and coding capabilities.

This illustration of Johannes Gutenberg is from an engraving on copper (1584), together with a page of Gutenberg's Bible.

The communications world of today has profited by the latest technology. Thousands of copies of full-color newspapers can be printed and collated in minutes. A skeleton staff can oversee the entire production at such newspresses where computers set the type (a photographic process) and correct errors.

It is clear that such technology has vastly reduced the size of the world. Events in a remote African village can be reported in New York almost the moment they occur.

7 · *The Future of Writing*

As we close the door on the twentieth century, sociologists tell us that we are about to be thrust into an unprecedented growth in information processing and global communications. Indeed, the signs of this phenomenon are already evident as we see multinational corporations restructuring their enterprises and developing global marketing strategies to promote the cross-fertilization of ideas between continents.

Multimedia news corporations aim to produce and distribute instant news throughout the world. Advertising agencies are receiving millions of dollars to produce one catchy sentence that can be sung or printed for a global audience. The communications wizards no longer believe in a world of multicultural villages; the global village concept has arrived.

It is rather sobering to realize that none of this would be possible but for the humble Sumerian clay tablet or the Canaanite invention of the alphabet. Without the universal acceptance and

We would do well to remember that behind today's advanced communication systems stands the ancient Sumerian inventor of writing.

recognition of the alphabet, computers, floppy discs, and communications satellites would have no meaning.

From an educational perspective, writing is here to stay. Not only does modern communications technology presuppose an understanding of writing and the alphabet, intellectual growth is uniquely linked to speech and writing. It is well known, for instance, that memory retention is enormously enhanced when written, spoken, and visual teaching methods are used together.

Humans will surely always have a compelling need to communicate on a personal level. Writing helps us describe events, unravel arguments, request information, answer questions, and generally share our intimate feelings.

As with all human endeavor, however, future generations will no doubt continue to adapt and modify writing to meet their changing needs. Meanwhile, archaeological exploration, assisted by ever-superior scientific methods of discovery and decipherment, will continue to shed valuable light on the origins of one of our greatest gifts from the past.

Index

Page numbers printed in *italic* type refer to illustrations.

Date Due

JAN 1 5 1989			

black sea

mediterranean sea